LOCAL RED BOOK

LEGEND

C000185082

.... way
.... ad
.... id
———— Road
———— rianized /
ted Access

========= Track

⌐ ⌐ Built Up Area

- - - - Footpath

∿∿ Stream

≈≈ River

≈Lock≈ Canal

—■— Railway / Station

● Post Office

🅿 🅿+☰ Car Park / Park & Ride

ⓒ Public Convenience

✚ Place of Worship

→ One-way Street

🅸 Tourist Information Centre

🔺8 🔺8 Adjoining Pages

▨ Area Depicting Enlarged Centre

▨ Emergency Services

▨ Industrial Buildings

▨ Leisure Buildings

▨ Education Buildings

▨ Hotels etc.

▨ Retail Buildings

▨ General Buildings

▨ Woodland

▨ Orchard

▨ Recreation Ground

▨ Cemetery

CONTENTS

Red Books showing the way

very effort has been made to verify the accuracy of information in this book but the ublishers cannot accept responsibility for expense or loss caused by an error or omission.

formation that will be of assistance to the user of the maps will be welcomed.

e representation on these maps of a road, track or path is no evidence of the existence of a ght of way.

reet plans prepared and published by ESTATE PUBLICATIONS, Bridewell House, ENTERDEN, KENT. The Publishers acknowledge the co-operation of the local authorities of wns represented in this atlas.

Ordnance Survey This product includes mapping data licensed from Ordnance Survey® with the permission of the Controller of Her Majesty's Stationery Office.

Crown Copyright
Estate Publications 492-06   ISBN 1 84192 374 5   All rights reserved
Licence number 100019031

www.ESTATE-PUBLICATIONS.co.uk

Printed by Ajanta Offset, New Delhi, India.

PAGE LAYOUT & ROAD MAP

Scale: 3 Miles to 1 Inc

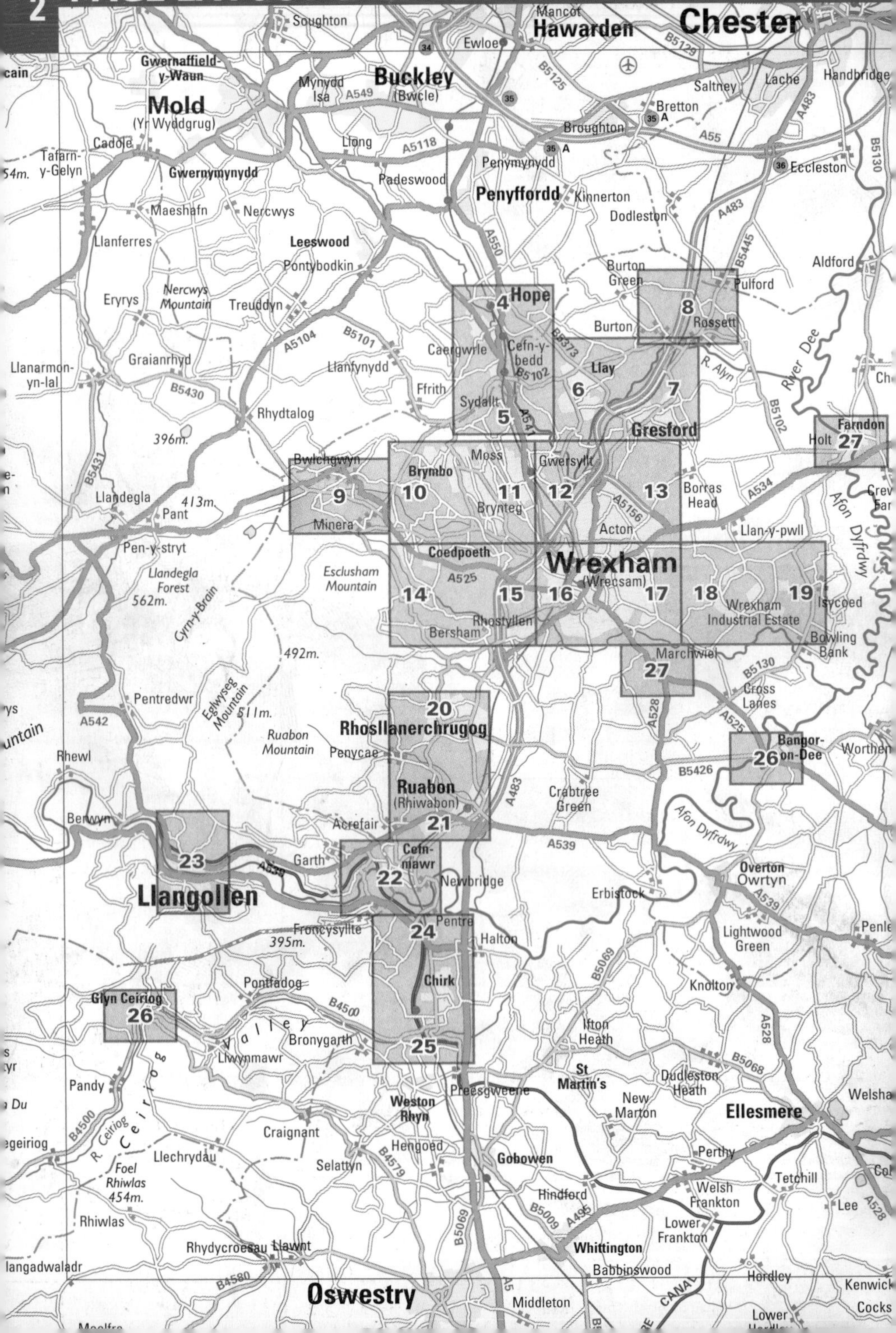
Soughton
Mancot
Hawarden
Chester
Ewloe
Gwernaffield-y-Waun
Buckley
(Bwcle)
Mynydd Isa
A549
Mold
(Yr Wyddgrug)
B5129
B5125
Saltney
Lache
Handbridge
Bretton
Broughton
A483
A55
A5118
Llong
Cadole
Tafarn-y-Gelyn
Gwernymynydd
Padeswood
Penymynydd
Penyffordd
Kinnerton
Dodleston
Eccleston
B5130
Maeshafn
Nercwys
Llanferres
Leeswood
Pontybodkin
A550
Burton Green
B5445
Pulford
Aldford
Eryrys
Nercwys Mountain
Treuddyn
Hope
Burton
Rossett
Graianrhyd
A5104
B5101
Caergwrle
Cefn-y-bedd
B5373
Llay
R. Alyn
River Dee
Llanarmon-yn-Ial
Llanfynydd
B5102
Ffrith
B5430
Rhydtalog
Sydallt
A541
Gresford
B5102
Farndon
Holt
396m.
Bwlchgwyn
Moss
Gwersyllt
Brymbo
Borras Head
A534
B5431
Llandegla
413m.
Pant
Minera
Brynteg
A5156
Acton
Llan-y-pwll
Afon Dyfrdwy
Pen-y-stryt
Coedpoeth
Wrexham
(Wrecsam)
Llandegla Forest
562m.
Esclusham Mountain
A525
Wrexham Industrial Estate
Isycoed
Cyrn-y-Brain
Rhostyllen
Bersham
Bowling Bank
492m.
Marchwiel
B5130
Cross Lanes
Pentredwr
Eglwyseg Mountain
511m.
A525
A542
Rhosllanerchrugog
Ruabon Mountain
Penycae
A528
Bangor-on-Dee
Worthen
Rhewl
B5426
Ruabon
(Rhiwabon)
A483
Crabtree Green
Afon Dyfrdwy
Berwyn
Acrefair
A539
Garth
Cefn-mawr
Overton
Owrtyn
A539
Newbridge
Llangollen
Erbistock
Pentre
Froncysyllte
395m.
Halton
Lightwood Green
Penley
B5069
Pontfadog
Chirk
Knolton
Glyn Ceiriog
B4500
Valley
Bronygarth
Ifton Heath
A528
Llwynmawr
B5068
St Martin's
Dudleston Heath
Pandy
Preesgweene
Weston Rhyn
New Marton
Ellesmere
Welsham
Ceiriog
B4500
R. Ceiriog
Craignant
Hengoed
Perthy
Llechrydau
B4579
Selattyn
Gobowen
Tetchill
Foel Rhiwlas
454m.
Hindford
Welsh Frankton
Lee
A528
B5009
A495
Lower Frankton
Rhiwlas
B5069
Rhydycroesau
Llawnt
Whittington
Llangadwaladr
Babbinswood
B4580
Hordley
Oswestry
A5
Middleton
CANAL
Kenwick
Cocks
Lower Hordley
4
5
6
7
8
9
10
11
12
13
14
15
16
17
18
19
20
21
22
23
24
25
26
27

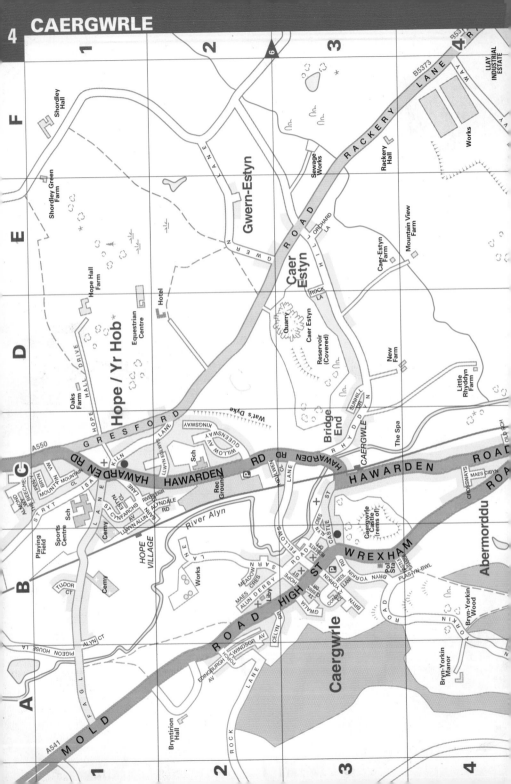

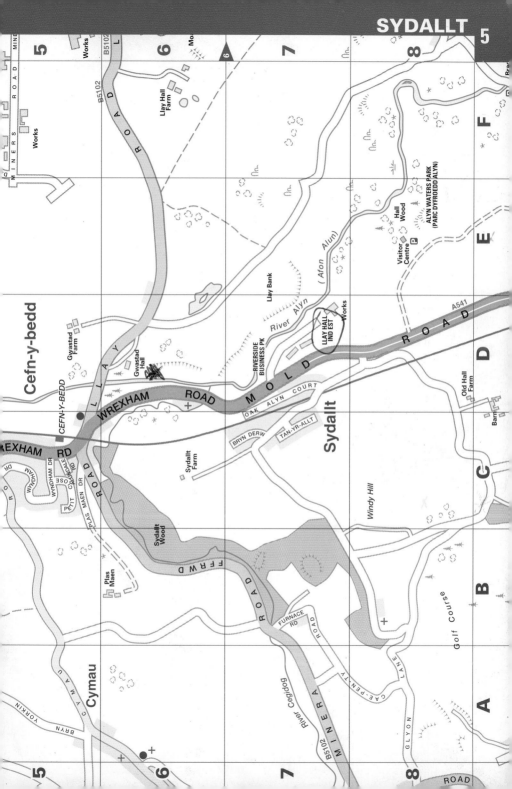

Cefn-y-bedd

Sydallt

Cymau

A map of Llay showing grid references A–D (columns) and 1–6 (rows).

Key locations and labels:

Row 1: DARK LANE, Quarry Bank Farm, Bank Farm, HIGHER LANE, CHAPEL COTTS, B5373, LANE WAY

Row 2: LLAY INDUSTRIAL ESTATE, Works, MINERS, RACKERY LANE, ROAD, MILE, STRAIGHT

Row 3: Works, Works, B5102, LLAY ROAD, GRESFORD ROAD, Home Farm, OLD MEADOW CT, Llay, Caravan Park, School, Health Centre, Sch, FAIROAKS, W BANK RD, PINFOLD LA, AERIAL RD, ACACIA CT, LINDEN GRO, WALNUT GRO, BOWEN GRO, FAIROAKS, FIRST AVENUE, SCHOOL ROAD, ST MARTINS MEWS, MEADOW, PINE GRO, FOREST, ELM, WILLOW DR, RISE, ASH GRO, Nant-y-gaer Wood, Sand and Pit (disus

Row 4: Sports Ground, Moat, Hall, Singret, Singrett Farm, Cockpit Wood, River Alyn (Afon Alun), Butts Hill, GRESFORD ROAD, LLAY AV, THIRD AV, SECOND AV, FIFTH AV, EIGTH AV, AVENUE, SEVENTH, FOURTH AV, HALL AV, OAK TREE AV, SIXTH, EIGHTH, NINTH AV, ELEVENTH AV, LABURNUM CT, Y-GAER, FFORDD GWENLLIAN, FFORDD TORVERTH, RHODFA'R GARN, MANOR, DYKE, LLYS, WATKIN RD, HUNTERS BROWFIELD, HARWOOD WY, LLAY NEW RD, BRYNFIELD, MADOCKS, FFORDD MABON, FFORDD MORGAN, PENDERYN WY, WATTS, SHONES, NANT Y GAER LANE, BEECH TREE, MAYFIELD CT, NEW HOUSE CT, BRYN PL, BRYN PL, PINGLE PL, VICTORY AV, BRON ALYN, Liby

Row 5: LLAY COUNTRY PARK, Golf Course, Golf Driving Range, Llay Cemetery, Worms Wood, TREWERYN CL, NEW ROAD, TENTH, LLAY CT, CROWN AVENUE, PENTRE, MAYVILLE AV, ST DAVIDS CRES, COUNCIL ST, STREET, PENTRE, VALE, VIEW, BRON ALYN, SPRINGFIELD, Cemetery, GRESFORD RD, CHURCH GRN, SCHOOL HILL, CLAPPERS LANE, La Fa

Row 6: Wats Dyke, Bradley Mill Bridge, BARRETTS HILL, LLAY NEW ROAD, B5425, PONT-Y-CAPEL, A483, PONT-Y-CAPEL LANE, Clapper Farm, Bradley, Tumulus, WFC, B5445, ROAD

12

F1 F2 F3 F4

Golf Course

OLD MEADOW
FAIR-

Darland Hall Farm

B5102
ROAD

CASTLE CT
PULFORD CT
BURDANEY CT
B5445 ROAD

Pulford

Playing Field

Motte & Bailey

Pulford Bridge

Sewage Works

COTTAGE LA
THE ORCHARDS

Darland Hall

Darland

GAMFORD LANE
BROADOAKS LANE
GAMFORD LANE

DARLAND

Playing Field

DODLESTON

Grosvenor Arms Hotel

CASTLE HILL LANE

WREXHAM

THE MILLYARD
ROSELANDS CT

LAVISTER
TWNS
DARLAND

ROAD

Lavister

Lavister Brook

School

WAVERLEY CRES
CHAPEL LANE
DARLAND VW
CROMAR CRES

TREVALYN HALL VW
Sch

RODENS
SHIRLEY LN
TREVALYN
WEST WY
GROSVENOR CRES

WAY

ALYN
GWYN ST
DRIVE
PARK CT
GLYN

A483

Broadoak Farm

ROSSETT BUSINESS VILLAGE

Llyndir Hall Hotel

LLYNDIR

Rossett (Yr Orsedd)

Rossett Hall Hotel

THE LIMES

CAMPBELL CL

MANOR

Marford

Cemy

HOLT CHESTER ROAD

THE COPSE

Rossett

Broadoak

Cam-yr-Alyn Farm

Balls Hall Farm

Burton Meadows

Burton House

Cam-yr-Alyn

BURTON ROAD
BARFIELDS
JOHNS CT
POPLAR ROW
STONEWALLS

Burton

ELM CT
STATION
Mill Rd
A483

LLAY ROAD

ROAD

Golden Grove PH

BURTON HALL LANE

ROSEMARY LANE

The Grange

Strathalyn

CROESHOWELL LANE
GREEN FLDS
SHOWELL
LLAY

Burton Hall

A1 A2 A3 A4

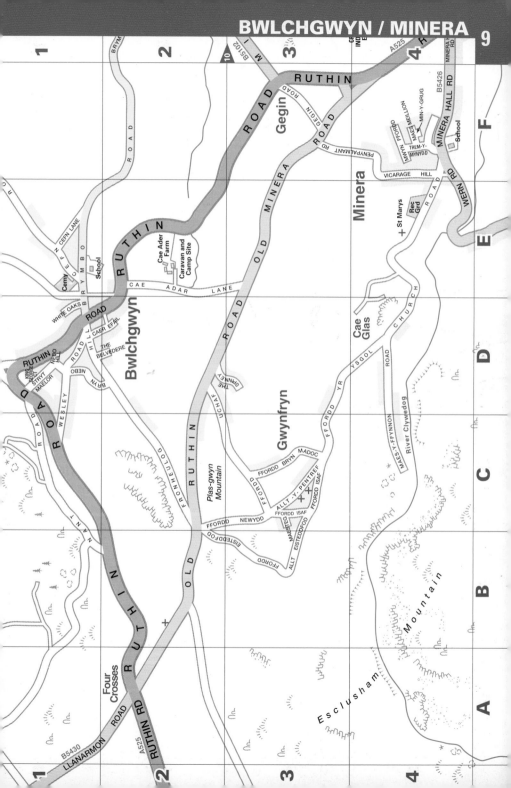

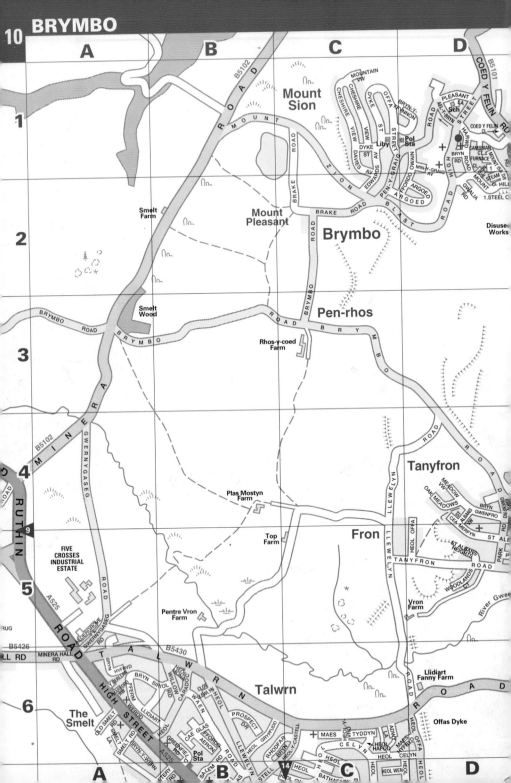

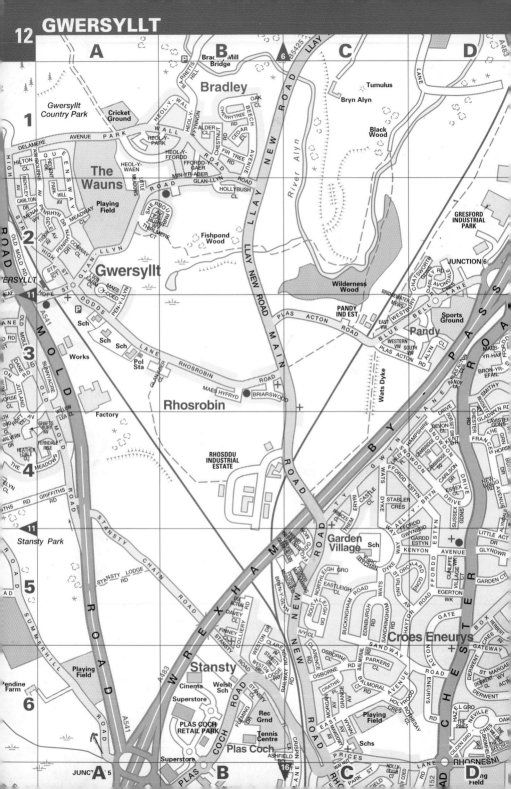

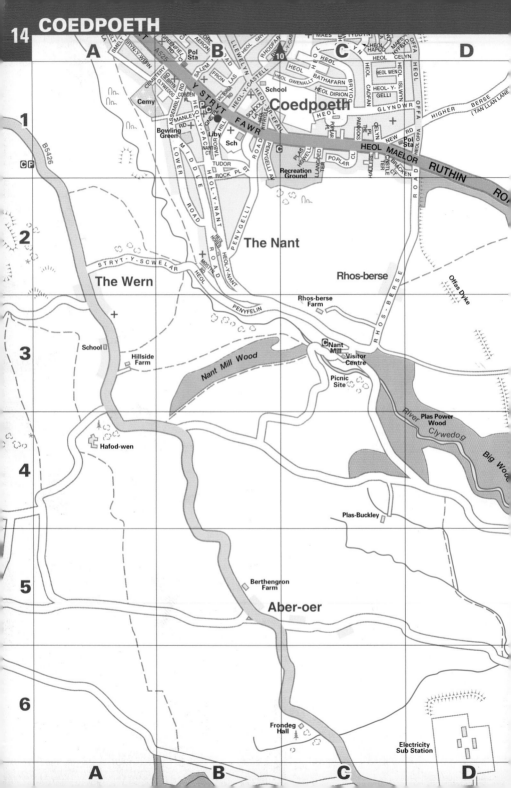

A **B** **C** **D**

1

2

3

4

5

6

Coedpoeth

The Nant

The Wern

Rhos-berse

Offa's Dyke

Rhos-berse Farm

School

Hillside Farm

Nant Mill Wood

Nant Mill

Visitor Centre

Picnic Site

River Clywedog

Plas Power Wood

Big Wood

Hafod-wen

Plas-Buckley

Berthengron Farm

Aber-oer

Frondeg Hall

Electricity Sub Station

Bowling Green

Recreation Ground

Cemetery

Pol Sta

Heol Maelor

Ruthin Road

B5426

Penyfelin

Penygelli

Heol-y-Nant

Stryt-y-Scwelar

Stryt Fawr

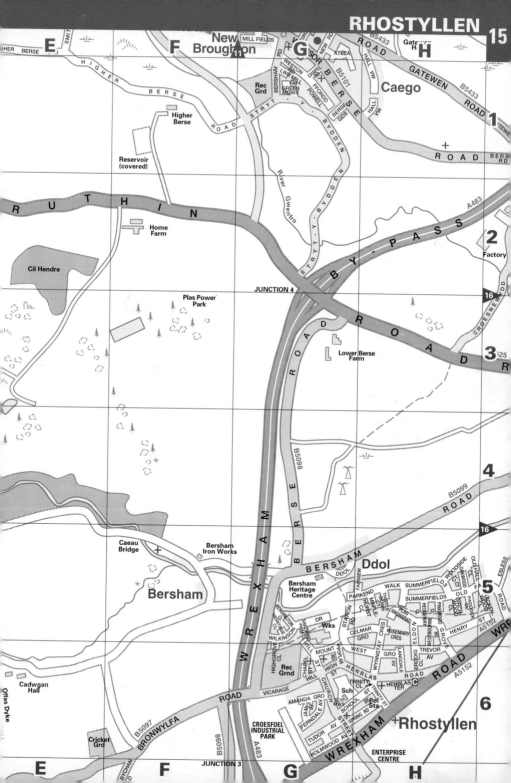

E F G H

New Broughton
MILL FIELDS
Caego
Gatewen
GATEWEN ROAD
B5433
SMIT
HIGHER BERSE
HIGHER BERSE
BERSE ROAD
Higher Berse
Reservoir (covered)
WESTON RD
BERSHAM
CHAPEL
LWR GN
MILL DDL
GREEN MDWS
NEW RD
ATLEA
HALL VW
HALL VW
Rec Grd
STRYT
SORBER
POWELL BERSE GDNS
FFORDD BYDDEN
B5101
ROAD
BERSE
BERS DD
ROAD
R U T H I N
Home Farm
River Gwenfro
STRYT - Y - BYDDEN
BY - PASS ROAD
A483
2
Factory
Cil Hendre
Plas Power Park
JUNCTION 4
ROAD
Lower Berse Farm
16
3
625
R
B5098
4
B5099 ROAD
16
Caeau Bridge
Bersham Iron Works
BERSHAM
DDOL
Bersham Heritage Centre
Ddol
WALK
SUMMERFIELD
WOODSIDE CL
OLD PADDOCK
OLD CHAPEL CT
ESLES
BERSE ROAD
WREXHAM ROAD
PARKEND
SUMMERFIELDS
MAPLE TRUST
PLAS ANGHARAD
HEDGEWAY
BIRCH GRO
PINEWOOD GRO
OLD PADDOCK CT
ROAD
A5152
5
Bersham
KENSINGTON CL
HIGHGROVE CL
WILKINSON ST
DR
Wks
STATION
CELMAR GRO
ROSEMARY CRES
WYNSTAY CRES
WESTBURY CL
ELDON
ERDDIG ROAD
LANGDALE
HENRY
TREVOR AV
WR
WREXHAM ROAD
A5152
MOUNT ST
CHAPEL HILL
HIGH ST
POPLAR ST
WEST
GRO
Rec Grnd
HENBLAS
HENBLAS TER
C
Cadwgan Hall
VICARAGE
CHURCH
TRINITY
ST TRINITY ST
Sch
SCHOOL
SPRING RD
Pol Sta
Rhostyllen
AMANDA GRO
JAMES ST
FERNDALE AV
Sch
SCHOOL AV
TUDOR
HOLMWOOD AV
CROESFOEL INDUSTRIAL PARK
WREXHAM ROAD
A483
ENTERPRISE CENTRE
Offa's Dyke
Cricket Grd
BRONWYLFA
B5097
B5608
JUNCTION 3

E F G H

6

Wrexham
Rugby Club

Sports Ground

Rhosnesni

Fox
Covert

Llwyn
Knottia

WREXHAM
(WRECSAM)

Cottage
Wood

Queensway
Sports Complex

Balloon Hill

e Dunks

Cefn Park

Sports
Ground

Works

WHITEGATE LIGHT
INDUSTRIAL ESTATE

Wks

School

Llwyn Onn
Hall

ntown

Kings Mill
Visitors
Centre

Kings Mills

Mill
Wood

Marchwes
Res

Bryn-newydd

Bryn-y-cabanau
Wood

Bryn-y-grog
Hall

Croes-y-m

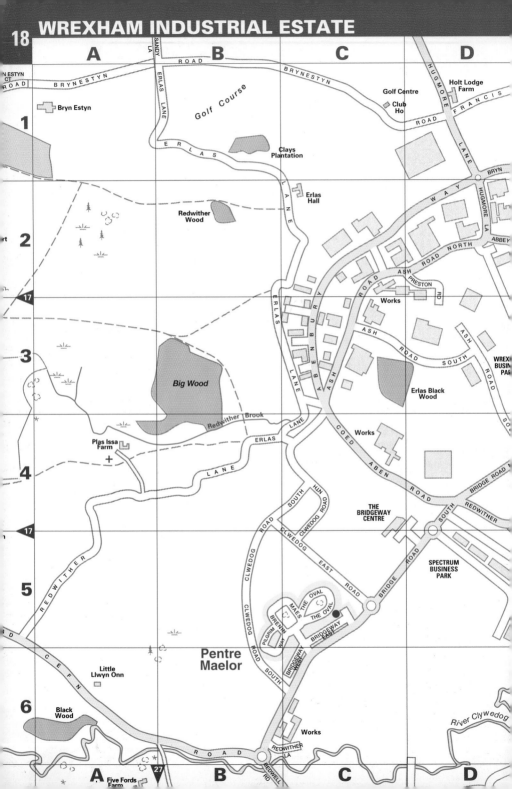

E   F   G   H

1

2

3

4

5

6

B5130

ROAD

Ridley Wood
Farm

RIDLEYWOOD

BRYN   LANE

N E

Works

Marshley
Farm

**WREXHAM
INDUSTRIAL ESTATE**

Isycoed

ABBEY CL

ELM

ROAD

FOURTH RD

OTHER
ESS
RE

AVENUE

ROAD

TOWER
CL

BRYN   LANE

Factory

SECOND   AVENUE

ROAD NORTH

ABBEY

Sch

BRIDGE

CHESTER ROAD

MARLBOROUGH
RD

ABBEY   ROAD

Depot

Factory

WITHER

ROAD

BRYN   LANE

OAK

Factory

ther   Brook

Bowling Bank
Farm

ROAD

Bowling
Bank

B5130

SUN   LANE

Mill
Wood

E   F   G   H

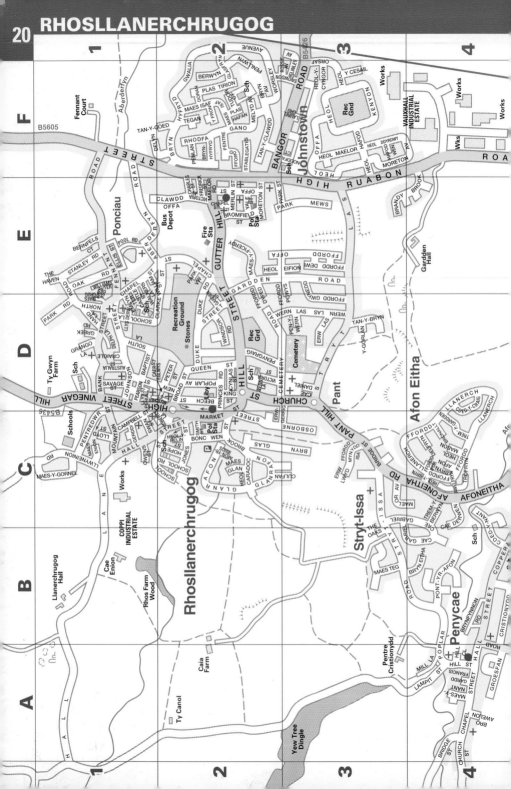

Wynnstay Park

Bathground Wood

Afon Eitha

Home Farm

VICARAGE FLDS
A539

F

Sch

JUNCTION 1

Caravan Site

James's Wood

E

B5605

D

Woodwards Rock

PLAS ISSA

SREEN

School

Pol Sta

Plas Madoc

DINAS
GLASLYN WY
OGWEN
HAMPDEN WY
GWYNANT
TEGID
WOODWARDS
WHALLEYS
AWEN
IDWAL
ALED
BRAN
BODLYN
Sports Centre
C

22

Plas-yn-Wern

Works

ROAD
ASH GRO
MAERN
MAPLE DR
OAK RD
COED RICHARD
WARE RIS
LANCASTER TER
HUGHES ROW
Playing Field
Sch
B

ROAD
PLAS BENNION
BENNION

Bryn Issa Farm

Works

BETHANIA
CHAPEL ST
HAWTHORNE AV
ERW DEG
DELPH ROW
L L A N G O L L E N

KING ST

Acrefair
Sch
BURTON TER
A539
A

Golf Course

Wynn Hall

Club Ho

ROAD
BENNION
Plas-Issa
DELPH ROAD
ROAD
A5097

5

Monks Pool

GARDDEN
NEWELL DR
RUABON ROAD
NEW HIGH ST
ROAD

Wks

GARDDEN IND EST

Pen-y-Gardden

Fort

Gardden Wood

Tatham Farm

Playing Field

Playing Field

Ruabon (Rhiwabon)

OLD SCHOOL CT
School
PONT ADAM
PONT ADAM CRES
Offa's Dyke

6

DANIEL S DR
BRYN WY
ALBERT GRO
NORTH AV
EAST AV
NEW WYNN AV
HALL

ST MICHAEL'S DR
BRYN ST
VINCENT ST
QUEEN ST
HENRY ST
ST
MAES-Y-LLAN

Cemy

ADAM

PONT

RUABON

ADAM CRES

STANLEY GRO
HAMBROOK GRO
ALBERT GRO
TY NEWYDD CT
Sch
JAY
HIGH ST
Surgery
Pol Sta
DENNIS
MADOC
CHURCH
BOWEN
ST
STATION TER
Sch

7

A483
BRIDGE ST
PARK ST
TANYLLAN
DUKE ST
CHURCH
THE PADDOCK
THE SPINNEY
THE BROOK
STATION RD
Station

ROAD

WYNNSTAY INDUSTRIAL ESTATE

8

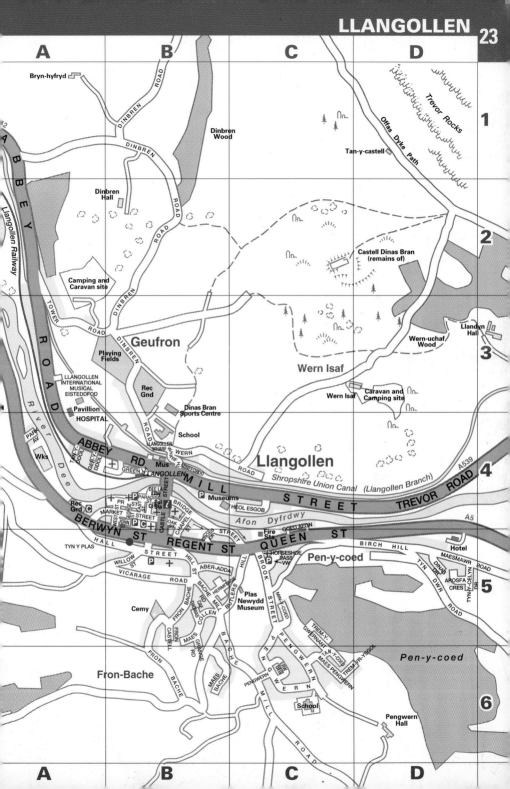

A **B** **C** **D**

Bryn-hyfryd

Trevor Rocks

1

Dinbren Wood

Offas Dyke Path

DINBREN ROAD

Tan-y-castell

DINBREN ROAD

Dinbren Hall

2

Castell Dinas Bran (remains of)

Llandyn Hall

Llangollen Railway

ABBEY ROAD

Camping and Caravan site

TOWER ROAD

DINBREN ROAD

Wern-uchaf Wood

3

Geufron

Playing Fields

Wern Isaf

Llandyn Hall

River Dee

LLANGOLLEN INTERNATIONAL MUSICAL EISTEDDFOD

Rec Gnd

Caravan and Camping site

Pavillion

HOSPITAL

Dinas Bran Sports Centre

Wern Isaf

PARK AV

Wks

School

ABBEY RD

LLANGOLLEN WHARF

Mus

WERN

Llangollen

A539

TREVOR ROAD

4

GREEN

LLANGOLLEN

MILL STREET

Shropshire Union Canal (Llangollen Branch)

A5

River Dee

GERY DDOL

DEE LA

PARADISE

Museums

HEOL ESGOB

BRIDGE

Afon Dyfrdwy

Rec Grd

MARKET

OAK ST

CHAPEL ST

CASTLE

CROSS STREET

Fire Stn

COED AFON

BIRCH HILL

Hotel

BERWYN ST

REGENT ST

QUEEN ST

HORSESHOE BASS

Pen-y-coed

MAESMAWR

ST

VW

TYN Y PLAS

HALL

WILLOW ST

VICARAGE ROAD

ABER-ADDA

HERMITAGE

BUTLERS HILL

HILL STREET

MILL STREET

PENGWERN BROOK

DINAS DWR ROAD

AROSFA CRES

TYN Y GELYN DR

5

Cemy

FRON BACHE

RD

FRON THOMAS CO

MAES GRANGE RD

BACHE MILL

Plas Newydd Museum

TREM Y GWERNANT

TAN-Y-COED

MAES PENGWERN

TREM Y-YSGOL

Pen-y-coed

FRON CASTELL

MAES BACHE

BACHE

Pengwern

PEN GWERN

Fron-Bache

FRON BACHE

MAES BACHE

MILL ROAD

School

6

Pengwern Hall

A **B** **C** **D**

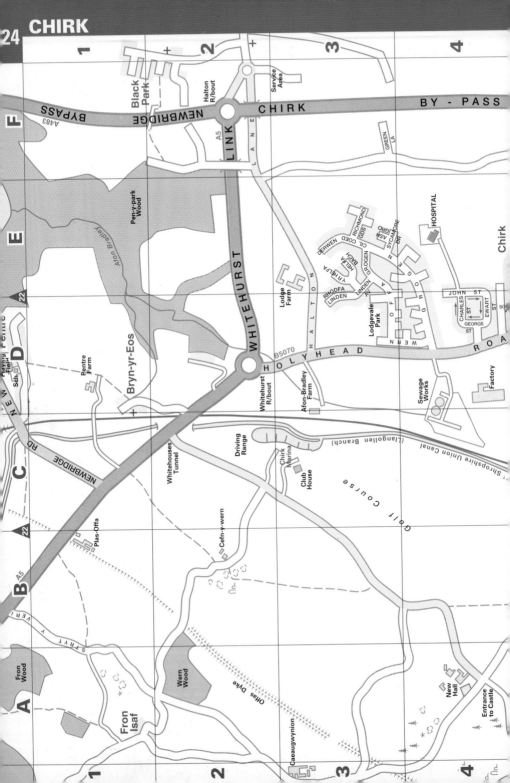

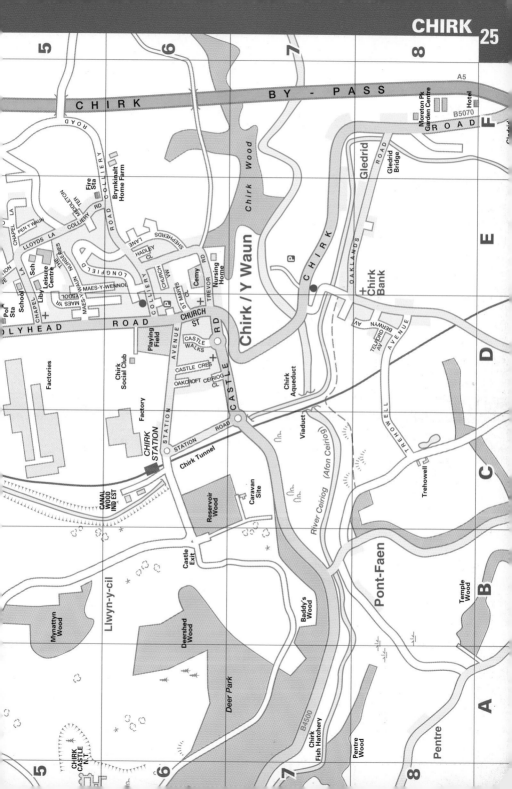

CHIRK BY - PASS

A5

Moreton Pk Garden Centre

Hotel

B5070

ROAD

F

Gledrid

Gledrid Bridge

E

Chirk Wood

CHIRK

Chirk / Y Waun

OAKLANDS

Chirk Bank

CHIRK BY - PASS

ROAD

COLLIERY

Brynkinalt Home Farm

Fire Sta

MIDDLETON

RD

SHEPHERDS LANE

HADLEY CL

NURSERIES

THE

CHAPEL LA

PEN Y WAUN

LLOYDS LA

Sch

Leisure Centre

School

Chapel

Lib

MAES YR YSGOL

MAES-Y-WENNOL

CHURCH VW

COLLIERY

LONGFIELD

CHURCH ST

ST MARYS CL

Cemy

TREVOR RD

Nursing Home

Pol Sta

HOLYHEAD ROAD

CHURCH ST

AVENUE

CASTLE WALKS

CASTLE CRES

OAKCROFT CEIRIOG CL

Playing Field

Chirk Social Club

Factories

Factory

STATION

CHIRK STATION

CASTLE RD

Chirk Aqueduct

TELFORD AV

BERWYN AV

TREHOWELL

AVENUE

D

Factory

CANAL WOOD IND EST

STATION ROAD

Chirk Tunnel

Reservoir Wood

Caravan Site

Viaduct

River Ceiriog (Afon Ceiriog)

Trehowell

C

Castle Exit

Mynattyn Wood

Llwyn-y-cil

Deershed Wood

Baddy's Wood

Pont-Faen

Temple Wood

B

Deer Park

B4500

Chirk Fish Hatchery

Pentre Wood

Pentre

A

CHIRK CASTLE N.T.

5   6   7   8

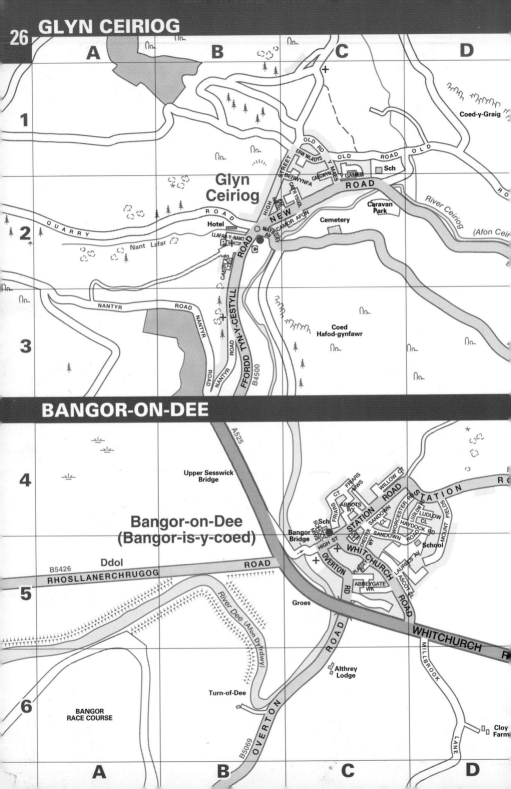

GLYN CEIRIOG

A **B** **C** **D**

1

Coed-y-Graig

OLD RD
ERW WLADYS
OLD ROAD
OLD
BERWYNFA
CAEGWYN
Y GAMEB
Sch
ROAD

Glyn
Ceiriog

CAER TSGOL
STREET
HIGH
River Ceiriog
Caravan
Park

QUARRY ROAD
Hotel
NEW
CAMOR AFON
Cemetery
(Afon Ceir

2
LLAFAR-Y-NANT
MAY-DUFFY
ROAD
Nant Lafar

CAE PLAS
ROAD

3
NANTYR ROAD
NANTYR
FFORDD TYN-Y-CESTYLL
ROAD
NANTYR
ROAD
Coed
Hafod-gynfawr
B4500

BANGOR-ON-DEE

A525

4
Upper Sesswick
Bridge
FRIARS
MWS
CT
WILLOW CT
STATION ROAD
FRIARS
ABBOTS
WY
WORCESTER RD
SANDOWN
CL
LUDLOW
CL
LUDLOW
HAYDOCK RD
MOUNT FIELD
SOLDEN
R

Bangor-on-Dee
(Bangor-is-y-coed)
Sch
STATION
SDCC
Bangor
Bridge
HIGH ST
CHESTER
WY
SANDOWN
ROAD
School
OVERTON
WHITCHURCH
LAURELS AV

Ddol
ROAD
B5426
RHOSLLANERCHRUGOG

5
River Dee (Afon Dyfrdwy)
Groes
RD
ABBEYGATE
WK
ASCOT CL
ROAD
WHITCHURCH
MILLBROOK
R

Althrey
Lodge

6
BANGOR
RACE COURSE
Turn-of-Dee
OVERTON
B5069
Cloy
Farm
LANE

A **B** **C** **D**

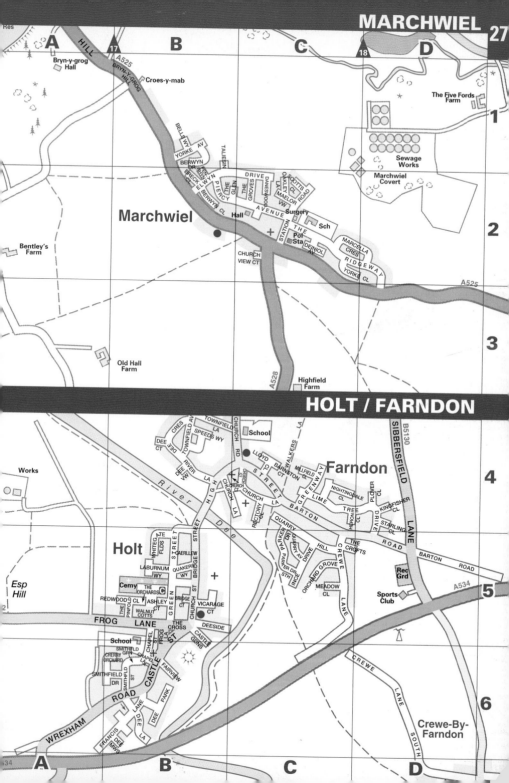

A **17** **B** **18** **C** **D**

Res

Bryn-y-grog Hall

HILL
A525
BRYN-Y-GROG HILL

Croes-y-mab

The Five Fords Farm

BELLS WY
YORKE AV
BERWYN DR
BRECON CT
ELWYN BERWYN CL
TALIESIN
PIERCY CL

Sewage Works

Marchwiel Covert

DRIVE
THE GROVES
DANESMOOR
OAKLEY LA
LA MAELOR WY
SCOTTS CL
OAKLEY ROAD
Surgery
Sch

Marchwiel

THE GLEN
THE AVENUE
Hall

STATION RD
Pol Sta
DEINIOL AV

MARCELLA CRES
RIDGEWAY
YORKE CL

1

Bentley's Farm

CHURCH VIEW CT

A525

2

Old Hall Farm

A528

Highfield Farm

3

Works

CRES
DEE CT
TOWNFIELD AV
TOWNFIELD LA
SPEEDS WY
CHURCH RD
School

WALKERS LA

River Dee
DEE WY
RIVER LA
HIGH STREET
CHURCH LA
CHURCHILL
RECTORY CL

LLOYD ST
BARNSTON CT
BARNSTON ROAD
GREENWAY
MILLFIELD CL

Farndon

SIBBERSFIELD LANE
B5130

4

Holt

WHITECROFTE FLDS
TE FLDS
CAERLLEW
STREET
QUAKERS WY
LABURNUM WY
REDWOOD CL
THE PINFOLD
Cemy
THE ORCHARDS
ASHLEY CT
WALNUT COTTS

GREEN ST
BRIDGE ST
CHURCH ST
VICARAGE CT

FROG LANE

DEESIDE

LIME
BARTON
NIGHTINGALE CL
TREE
HERON LA
QUARRY LA
PARKER DRIVE
QUARRY AV
PARKER DR STH

HILL DRIVE
ORCHARD GROVE
INCE AV
MEADOW CL

THE CROFTS
CREWE LANE

PLOVER CL
STARLING CL
KINGFISHER CL
ROAD
THE CROFTS

BARTON ROAD

A534

5

Esp Hill

School

SMITHFIELD GRN
CHERRY ORCHARD
SMITHFIELD DR

CHAPEL LA
FROG LA
CASTLE ST
THE CROSS
FAIRVIEW
CASTLE GDNS
DEE PARK
DEE LA
FRANCIS DR MWS

WREXHAM ROAD

Rec Grd

Sports Club

CREWE LANE

CREWE LANE SOUTH

Crewe-By-Farndon

6

A **B** **C** **D**

A - Z INDEX TO STREETS
with Postcodes

The Index includes some names for which there is insufficient space on the maps. These names are indicated by an * and are followed by the nearest adjoining thoroughfare.

Aarons Rd LL11 11 G4
Abbey Cl LL13 19 E2
Abbey Rd, Llangollen LL20 23 A1
Abbey Rd, Wrexham LL13 18 D2
Abbeydale Cl LL13 13 H6
Abbeygate Walk LL13 26 C5
Abbot St LL11 3 C4
Abbots Way LL13 26 C5
Abenbury Rd LL13 17 F5
Abenbury Way LL13 18 C3
Aber Adda LL20 23 B5
Aberderfyn Rd LL14 20 E1
Acacia Ct LL12 6 A3
Acton Gate LL11 12 D6
Acton Gdns LL12 13 E5
Acton Llan Y Pwll Link Rd LL12 13 E3
Acton Park Way LL12 12 D6
Acton Rd LL11 16 C1
Adderley Bank LL11 12 D3
Adwy La LL11 10 C6
Ael y Bryn, Brymbo LL11 10 D1
Ael y Bryn, Wrexham LL11 12 C4
Aerial Rd LL12 6 A3
Afon Yr Rhos LL14 20 C2
Afoneitha Rd LL14 20 D2
Ainsdale Gro LL12 13 G5
Airoaks Cres LL12 6 B3
Albert St LL13 3 D5
Alder Cl LL11 12 D6
Aldford Way LL12 13 F6
Aldergrove LL11 10 A5
Aled LL14 21 C7
Alexandra Rd LL13 3 A5
Allington Cres LL12 7 E6
Allington Dr LL13 17 F2
Allt Eisteddfod LL11 9 B3
Allt y Pentref LL11 9 C3
Alma Rd LL20 22 A4
Almond Gro LL13 17 F1
Alundale Rd LL12 5 C5
Alun LL14 21 C8
Alwen Cl LL11 11 G6
Alyn Cl LL11 12 D3
Alyn Cres LL12 4 B3
Alyn Ct LL12 4 A1
Alyn Dr LL12 8 D4
Alyndale Rd, Hope LL12 4 C1
Alyndale Rd, Wrexham LL12 12 D5
Amanda Gro LL14 15 G6
Anglesey Cl LL12 13 F6
Annefield Pk LL12 7 G3
Ansell Rd LL13 13 G5
Anthony Eden Dr LL13 17 F3
Applewood LL13 16 D5
Aran Rd LL12 17 E1
Archers Way LL13 17 E2
Arenig Cl LL11 11 H4
Arenig Rd LL13 17 G3
Arfryn LL11 11 F5
Argoed LL11 10 C2
Argyle St LL13 3 C3
Arley Rd LL11 12 D2
Arosfa Cres LL20 23 D5
Ascot Cl LL13 26 C5
Ash Cl LL11 11 G1
Ash Gro, Acrefair LL14 21 B8
Ash Gro, Chirk LL14 24 E3
Ash Gro, Llay LL12 6 C3
Ash Gro, Wrexham LL13 17 F1
Ash Rd LL13 18 C2
Ash Rd North LL13 18 C2
Ash Rd South LL13 18 C3
Ashbourne Av LL11 11 H1
Ashburn Way LL13 17 F4
Ashfield Rd LL12 12 B6
Ashley Ct LL13 27 B6
Assembly Rd LL13 14 B1
Aston Gro LL12 17 E1
Atlea LL11 11 G6
Augusta Dr LL13 13 G6
Australia St LL14 20 D1
Avalon Ct LL13 16 D5

Avon Cl LL12 13 E6
Avon Dale Gro LL12 13 G5
Avondale Cres LL11 12 D2
Awelfryn LL14 20 C4

Bache Mill Rd LL20 23 B5
Bader Ct LL13 13 G5
Bakery Flds LL11 11 G5
Bala Rd LL13 17 G3
Balmoral Cl LL13 12 C6
Balmoral Rd LL11 12 C6
Bangor Rd LL14 20 F2
Bank St, Ponciau LL14 20 D1
Bank St, Southsea LL11 11 E6
Bank St, Wrexham LL11 3 C3
Baptist St LL14 20 D1
Barkers La LL12 13 E4
Barnfelde La LL12 8 B3
Barnfield LL13 3 C5
Barnston Ct CH3 27 C4
Barons Rd LL14 17 E3
Barretts Hill LL11 12 B1
Barter Ct LL13 17 E5
Barter Rd LL13 17 E5
Barton Cl LL13 16 D6
Barton Rd CH3 27 C4
Bath Rd LL13 3 B5
Beacon Rd LL11 11 H4
Bedevere Ct LL13 16 D5
Beech Av, Bradley LL11 12 B1
Beech Av, Gresford LL12 7 E5
Beech Gdns LL13 3 D5
Beech St, Rhosllanerchrugog LL14 20 D2
Beech St, Summerhill LL11 11 G1
Beech Tree Av LL12 6 B4
Beechley Rd LL13 3 D6
Belfry Cl LL13 13 H6
Belgrave Ct LL12 7 F5
Belgrave Rd LL13 3 C6
Bell Ct LL13 17 E5
Bellevue Ct LL13 3 B4
Bellevue Rd LL13 3 A4
Bells Way LL13 27 B1
Belmont Rd LL13 3 B6
Belvedere Dr LL11 16 A1
Benjamin Pl LL13 17 E3
Benjamin Rd LL13 17 E3
Bennetts Rd LL11 11 F2
Bennions Rd LL13 14 B5
Bentley Av LL11 11 H1
Bernard Rd LL13 17 E3
Bernfels Ct LL14 20 E1
Berse Gdns LL11 15 G1
Berse Rd, Bersham LL14 15 G5
Berse Rd, New Broughton LL11 15 G1
Bersham Rd, Bersham LL14 15 G5
Bersham Rd, New Broughton LL11 15 G1
Bersham Rd, Wrexham LL13, 14 3 A5
Bertie Rd LL13 17 E3
Berwyn LL14 20 F2
Berwyn Av LL14 25 D8
Berwyn Cl LL13 27 B2
Berwyn Dr LL13 27 B1
Berwyn St LL20 23 A4
Berwyn Vw LL13 17 G3
Berwynfa LL20 26 C1
Bethania Rd LL14 21 A8
Beverley Cl LL13 17 G5
Bickerton Dr LL11 11 H3
Bickleywood Dr LL13 17 F1
Bieston Cl LL13 13 F4
Birch Dr LL12 7 F5
Birch Hill LL20 23 D5
Birch St LL13 3 D5
Birch Tree Cl LL11 11 G5
Birchwood Cl LL14 15 H5
Birkdale Cl LL13 13 G6
Birkdale Rd LL13 13 G6
Blacklane Rd LL11 11 F2
Blackthorn Cl LL13 17 F5
Blantern Way LL13 13 G6
Blast Rd LL11 10 C2
Blue Bell La LL11 12 C3
Bodhyfryd LL13 3 D2
Bodlyn LL14 21 C7
Bodwyn Cres LL12 7 E6
Bodwyn Pk LL12 7 E6
Bonc Wen LL14 20 C2

Border Retail Pk LL13 16 D2
Borras Park Rd LL12,13 13 F6
Borras Rd LL12 17 E1
Bottom Rd LL11 11 G1
Bowen Ct LL14 21 F7
Bowens La LL14 22 D2
Box La LL12 12 D5
Bracken Ct LL13 14 C1
Brackenwood Cl LL14 16 A5
Bradley Rd LL13 3 B3
Braeside LL13 17 G5
Brake Rd, Brymbo LL11 10 C2
Brake Rd, Moss LL11 11 F2
Bramble Cl LL12 7 G5
Bran LL14 21 C7
Brandon Gro LL12 8 D4
Brandy Brook LL14 20 E3
Breck Cl LL13 27 B2
Brecon Cl LL12 13 F6
Brewery Pl LL13 3 B3
Briarswood LL11 12 B3
Bridge Ct, Holt LL13 27 B5
Bridge Ct, Southsea LL11 11 E6
Bridge Rd North LL13 18 D4
Bridge Rd South LL13 18 C5
Bridge St, Holt LL13 27 B5
Bridge St, Llangollen LL20 23 B4
Bridge St, Pant, Penycae LL14 20 C3
Bridge St, Penycae LL14 20 A4
Bridge St, Ruabon LL14 21 F7
Bridge St, Southsea LL11 11 E6
Bridge St, Wrexham LL13 3 C4
Bridgewater Mws LL11 12 C2
Bridgeway East LL13 18 C5
Bridgeway West LL13 18 C6
Bright St LL13 3 A4
Bro Awelon LL14 20 A4
Bro Gwilym LL14 22 D2
Broad St LL14 20 D2
Broadoaks LL12 8 E3
Bromfield Av LL12 6 A4
Bromfield Gro LL12 12 D6
Bromfield St LL14 20 E2
Bron Alyn LL12 6 C5
Bron y Coed LL13 3 A6
Bron y Dre LL13 3 A6
Bron y Gamlas LL20 22 B2
Bron y Nant LL13 16 B2
Bron yr Efail LL12 12 D3
Bronallt LL14 20 C4
Bronwylfa Rd LL14 15 F6
Brook Cl LL13 17 G5
Brook St, Llangollen LL20 23 C5
Brook St, Rhosllanerchrugog LL14 20 C2
Brook St, Rhosymedre LL14 22 E1
Brook St, Wrexham LL13 3 A5
Broom Gro LL13 17 F2
Broughton Rd LL11 11 E4
Browns La LL14 22 D1
Broxton Rd LL13 17 F2
Brymbo Link Rd LL11 11 E5
Brymbo Rd LL11 9 D1
Bryn Afon LL14 20 C4
Bryn Av LL14 20 F2
Bryn Awel LL11 11 G6
Bryn Celyn,
Bryn Celyn, Moss LL11 11 F5
Bryn Clywedog LL11 14 B1
Bryn Coed LL11 11 G2
Bryn Derw LL12 5 C7
Bryn Eglwys Rd LL13 17 G3
Bryn Eitha LL14 20 B4
Bryn Eryl LL20 20 C3
Bryn Estyn Rd LL13 17 H1
Bryn Ffynnon LL13 3 C3
Bryn Fynnon Rd LL14 20 B4
Bryn Glas LL14 20 C3
Bryn Glas LL11 11 H2
Bryn Goleu LL11 11 F5
Bryn Gro LL13 17 G1
Bryn Gryffydd LL12 13 F5
Bryn Gwenfro LL11 10 D4
Bryn Hafod LL13 17 F4

Bryn Hedd LL11 11 F5
Bryn Hyfryd,
Bryn Hyfryd, Coedpoeth LL11 10 A6
Bryn Hyfryd, Johnstown LL14 20 F2
Bryn La LL13 18 D1
Bryn Maelor LL11 11 F5
Bryn Nebo LL11 9 D2
Bryn Pl LL12 6 C4
Bryn Rd, Brymbo LL11 10 D1
Bryn Rd, Moss LL11 11 F1
Bryn Rhedyn LL11 11 F6
Bryn Siriol LL11 10 A6
Bryn St LL14 21 F6
Bryn Way LL14 21 F5
Bryn y Barcut LL14 20 B4
Bryn y Cabanau Rd LL13 3 D5
Bryn y Ffynnon LL11 10 D1
Bryn y Gaer Rd LL11 11 F3
Bryn y Glyn LL12 12 B5
Bryn y Grog Hill LL13 27 A1
Bryn y Wern LL11 10 A6
Bryn Ydd LL14 20 D1
Bryn Yorkin LL12 4 B3
Bryn Yorkin Rd LL12 5 A5
Bryn yr Onnen LL11 11 F5
Bryncoed Rd LL11 11 F1
Bryndraw Ter LL13 3 C4
Brynestyn Rd LL13 17 G1
Brynisa Rd LL11 11 G4
Brynteg Cres LL11 11 F3
Buckingham Rd LL11 12 C5
Burganey Ct CH4 8 E1
Burnham Gdns LL11 17 F3
Burton Dr LL12 12 D4
Burton Hall Rd LL12 8 A2
Burton Rd LL12 8 B3
Burton Rise LL12 7 F5
Bury St LL13 3 D5
Butcher St LL14 20 D1
Butlers Hill LL20 23 B5

Cae Adar La LL11 9 E2
Cae Coch La LL14 22 D1
Cae Daniel LL14 20 D3
Cae Derwen LL14 20 C4
Cae Gabriel LL14 20 B4
Cae Glas LL11 10 B6
Cae Gwilym La LL14 22 D2
Cae Gwilym Rd LL14 22 D3
Cae Hafod LL20 26 B2
Cae Merfyn LL11 10 D4
Cae Pentre LL11 11 F4
Cae Penty Rd LL12 5 A8
Cae Plas Teg LL20 26 B2
Cae Thomas LL20 23 B5
Caegwyn LL20 26 C2
Cae Efail LL11 9 D1
Caer Eglwys LL14 20 D1
Caer Haf LL11 11 G1
Caer Llan LL14 21 F6
Caer Ysgol LL20 26 C2
Caerllew LL13 27 B5
Caernavon Rd LL12 13 F6
Caia Gdns LL13 17 E3
Caia Rd LL13 3 D4
Camberley Dr LL12 17 E1
Camberley Rise LL12 17 E1
Cambrian LL11 10 D1
Cambridge Sq LL11 12 D6
Camor Afon LL20 26 C2
Campbell Cl LL12 8 D4
Campbell St LL11 20 C1
Canal Wood Ind Est LL14 25 C5
Cappers Hill LL11 11 G4
Carden Park Way LL13 13 G6
Cardigan Rd LL12 13 F6
Carlson Dr LL11 12 D4
Carlton Dr LL11 11 H2
Carnoustie Cl LL13 17 H1
Cartmel Cl LL13 17 F5
Castle Cl, Chester CH4 8 F1
Castle Cl, Wrexham LL11 12 C4
Castle Cres LL14 25 D6
Castle Gdns LL13 27 B5
Castle Grange LL12 4 B4
Castle Hill CH4 8 E1
Castle Rd LL14 25 D7
Castle St, Caergwrle LL12 4 C4
Castle St, Holt LL13 27 B6
Castle St, Llangollen LL20 23 B5

Castle St, Ponciau LL14 20 D1
Castle Ter LL11 14 C1
Castle Walks LL14 25 D6
Castletown Rd LL11 11 F2
Cavendish Ct LL12 7 F5
Cavendish Sq LL12 13 E4
Caxton Pl LL13 3 B2
Cedar Cl, Bradley LL11 12 B1
Cedar Cl, Gresford LL12 7 F6
Cedar Cl, Wrexham LL12 13 F4
Cedar Dr LL11 12 C5
Cefn La LL11 9 E1
Cefn Parc*, Stryt Issa LL14 20 B3
Cefn Rd, Brynteg LL11 11 E3
Cefn Rd, Bwlchgwyn LL11 9 E1
Cefn Rd, Wrexham LL13 17 G1
Cefn y Bedd LL12 5 C5
Cefndre LL13 17 G4
Ceiriog Cl LL14 25 D6
Ceiriog Rd LL13 17 G3
Celmar Gro LL14 15 G5
Celyn Cl LL11 11 H4
Celyn Dr LL12 4 B2
Celyn Pl LL11 14 C1
Cemetery Rd, Coedpoeth LL11 14 A1
Cemetery Rd, Rhosllanerchrugog LL14 20 D3
Centenary Rd LL13 16 A4
Central Av LL12 13 E6
Central Rd LL13 3 A2
Cerney Rd LL11 11 F1
Chanticleer Cl LL13 17 F1
Chapel Ct LL11 11 E6
Chapel La, Chirk LL14 25 D5
Chapel La, Holt LL13 27 B6
Chapel La, Llay LL12 6 B2
Chapel La, Rossett LL12 8 D3
Chapel Pl LL13 3 B5
Chapel Rd LL11 15 G1
Chapel St, Acrefair LL14 21 A8
Chapel St, Holt LL13 27 B6
Chapel St, Johnstown LL14 20 E2
Chapel St, Llangollen LL20 23 B5
Chapel St, Penycae LL14 20 A4
Chapel St, Rhostyllen LL14 15 G6
Chapel St, Rhosymedre LL14 22 E1
Chapel St, Wrexham LL13 3 C4
Charles Av LL20 22 B1
Charles St, Chirk LL14 24 D4
Charles St, Johnstown LL14 20 E2
Charles St, Wrexham LL13 3 D4
Chatsworth Dr LL11 11 H4
Chatsworth Gdns LL11 12 D2
Chelston Av LL13 13 F4
Chepstow La LL13 17 G5
Cherry Fld LL11 11 G5
Cherry Hill Dr LL12 13 F5
Cherry Orch LL13 27 B6
Cherrytree Rd LL11 12 B1
Cheshire Av LL13 3 D4
Cheshire Vw, Brymbo LL11 10 C1
Cheshire Vw, Wrexham LL13 17 E2
Chester Rd, Rossett LL12 7 G2
Chester Rd, Wrexham LL11,12 3 D1
Chester St LL13 3 D3
Chester Way LL13 26 C5
Chestnut Av, Summerhill LL11 11 G1
Chestnut Av, Wrexham LL11,12 12 D5
Chestnut Cl LL12 7 E5
Chestnut Cl LL11 11 G3
Chestnut Rd LL11 12 B1
Chetwyn Ct LL12 7 F5
Cheviot Cl LL11 11 H4
Chiltern Cl LL11 11 H4
Chirk Rd LL14 25 E7
Church Ct CH3 27 B4

Church Grn LL12 6 D5
Church La CH3 27 B4
Church Rd, Brynteg LL11 11 G4
Church Rd, Farndon CH3 27 C4
Church Rd, Minera LL11 9 D4
Church Rd, Southsea LL11 11 E6
Church St, Farndon CH3 27 C4
Church St, Gwersyllt LL11 11 H2
Church St, Holt LL13 27 B5
Church St, Penycae LL14 20 A4
Church St, Rhosllanerchrugog LL14 20 D3
Church St, Rhostyllen LL14 15 G6
Church St, Rhosymedre LL14 22 E1
Church St, Ruabon LL14 21 F7
Church St, Wrexham LL13 3 C4
Church View Ct LL13 27 C2
Church Vw, Chirk LL14 25 E6
Church Vw, Ruabon LL14 21 E7
Churchill Dr LL13 17 F2
Churton Dr LL13 17 E2
Cil Coed LL14 24 E3
Cilcen Gro LL12 12 D6
Cileen LL11 11 G1
Clappers La LL12 6 D5
Clarence Rd LL11 12 C6
Clarendon Av LL11 12 B5
Clarke Rd LL12 13 F5
Clarke St LL14 20 D2
Clawdd Offa LL14 20 E2
Claypit La LL12 7 F5
Clayton Rd LL11 11 E1
Cleveland St LL14 21 F6
Clifton Cl LL13 17 E4
Clos Ascot LL13 17 G5
Clos Llewelyn LL11 10 B6
Clos Ystrad LL13 16 C5
Clwedog East Rd LL13 18 B4
Clwedog Rd North LL13 18 C5
Clwedog Rd South LL13 18 B5
Clwyd Wen LL13 17 E4
Clywedog Cl LL11 11 H4
Cobden Pl LL11 14 B1
Cobden Rd LL13 3 A3
Cobham Cl LL13 16 D6
Coed Aben LL13 17 G3
Coed Aben Rd LL13 18 C4
Coed Afon LL20 23 C5
Coed Efa La LL11 11 G5
Coed Richard LL14 21 B8
Coed y Bryn LL13 17 G4
Coed y Felin Cl LL11 10 D1
Coed y Felin Rd LL11 10 D1
Coed y Ffynnon LL13 16 C5
Coed y Graig LL14 20 D4
Coed y Nant, Penycae LL14 20 B4
Coed y Nant, Wrexham LL13 16 C5
Colemere St LL13 3 B5
College Hill LL11 11 E5
College St LL13 3 C4
Colliery Rd, Chirk LL14 25 D6
Colliery Rd, Southsea LL11 11 E5
Colliery Rd, Wrexham LL11 12 B6
Collins Ct LL13 17 E5
Colwyn Rd LL13 17 E3
Concorde Row LL13 13 G5
Coningsby Ct LL13 13 G5
Connor Cres LL13 17 E4
Conway Cl, Caergwrle LL12 4 B3
Conway Cl, Gwersyllt LL11 12 A2
Conway Dr LL13 17 G2
Coopers Cl LL13 17 F1
Copperas Hill LL14 20 B4
Coppi Ind Est LL14 20 B1
Cornish Cl LL13 16 D5
Coronation Dr LL14 25 E5
Coronation St, Cefn-mawr LL14 22 D3
Coronation St, New Broughton LL11 11 G6
Cosford Cl LL13 13 G5
Cottage Cl LL12 8 F2
Council St LL12 6 B4
Court Rd LL13 3 A6
Cox La LL12 7 G4
Craig Cl LL14 25 E5
Craig Way LL12 13 E6
Craigle LL14 20 D1
Craigmillar Cl LL12 3 D1
Crane St LL14 22 D2
Cranford Rd LL13 17 F2
Crathie Pl LL11 12 C6
Crescent Cl LL13 17 E2
Crescent Rd LL13 3 D3
Crewe La CH3 27 C5
Crewe La South CH3 27 C6
Cripps Av LL11 11 F6
Crispin La LL11 3 A1
Cristionydd LL14 20 B4
Croesfoel Ind Pk LL14 15 G6
Croeshowell Hill LL12 7 E1
Croeshowell La LL12 7 E1
Croesnewydd Rd LL13 3 A3
Cromar Cres LL12 8 E3
Cross La, Llangollen LL20 23 B5
Cross La, Wrexham LL11 11 F3
Cross St, Southsea LL11 11 F6
Cross St, Wrexham LL11 3 C1
Crossways, Caergwrle LL12 4 C4
Crossways, Wrexham LL13 17 E2
Crown Pl LL12 6 B4
Culfan LL14 20 C3
Cunliffe St LL11 3 C1
Cunliffe Walk LL11 12 D5
Cunningham Av LL13 17 E2
Cwm Eithin LL12 13 E3
Cymau Rd LL12 5 A5
Cynlas LL11 11 F5
Cynlas St LL14 20 D2

Daisy Bank Cl LL14 16 A4
Daisy Rd LL11 11 G4
Dale Ct LL11 11 G6
Dale Rd LL11 11 G6
Dale St LL13 17 E3
Daleside Av LL12 13 G5
Dane Cl LL11 11 H3
Daneswood LL13 27 C2
Daniels Dr LL14 21 F5
Darby Rd LL11 11 F5
Darland Cl LL12 8 E3
Darland La LL12 8 E2
Darland Vw LL12 8 E3
Davey Cl LL11 12 B5
Davies Av LL11 10 C1
Davies Ct LL13 17 E5
Davy Way LL12 5 F5
Ddol LL14 15 G5
Dean Cl LL13 13 F6
Dean Rd LL13 13 F6
Dee Av LL12 13 E6
Dee Cres CH3 27 B4
Dee Ct, Chester CH3 27 B4
Dee Ct, Wrexham LL13 26 C5
Dee La, Llangollen LL20 23 B4
Dee La, Wrexham LL13 27 B6
Dee Mdws LL13 27 B6
Dee Pk LL13 27 B6
Dee Vw CH3 27 B4
Deeside LL13 27 B5
Deiniol Av LL13 27 C2
Delamere Av LL11 11 H1
Delfryn LL14 20 C4
Delph La LL14 20 D1
Delph Rd LL14 21 A5
Delyn LL14 20 F2
Denbigh Cl LL12 13 F6
Denning Rd LL12 13 F5
Dennis Ct LL14 21 F7
Derby Rd, Caergwrle LL12 4 B2
Derby Rd, Wrexham LL13 16 D3
Derwen LL14 24 E3
Derwent Cl LL12 12 D6
Derwent Cres LL12 12 D6
Deva Way LL13 17 F2
Devon Cl LL11 12 D4
Dinas LL14 21 C8
Dinas Dr LL20 23 D5
Dinbren Rd LL20 23 B1
Dingle Pl LL12 6 B4
Dodds La LL11 12 A3
Dodleston La CH4 8 E1
Dol Acton LL11 12 B5
Dolydd La LL14 22 C2
Dolydd Rd, Cefn-mawr LL14 22 D2
Dolydd Rd, Wrexham LL13 3 A3
Doran LL14 20 F2
Dorset Dr LL11 12 D4
Drws y Coed LL13 16 C6
Duke Rd LL14 20 D2
Duke St, Chirk LL14 25 D5
Duke St, Rhosllanerchrugog LL14 20 D2
Duke St, Ruabon LL14 21 F7
Duke St, Wrexham LL11 3 B3
Dunster Rd LL13 19 E4
Dutton Rd LL13 19 E3
Dyke St LL11 10 C1

Eagle Mdw LL13 3 D4
Eagles Pl LL11 11 F2
Earle St LL13 3 C5
East Av, Ruabon LL14 21 F6
East Av, Wrexham LL11 12 C6
East St LL20 23 B4
East Vw LL11 12 C3
Eastfield Ct LL13 17 G5
Eastleigh Cl LL11 12 C5
Eaton Cl LL12 8 E4
Eaton Dr LL13 17 F2
Edinburgh Rd LL11 12 C5
Edingburgh Av LL12 4 A2
Edward St LL13 3 A5
Edwards Av LL11 10 C2
Egerton St LL11 3 C3
Egerton Walk LL11 12 D5
Eglwysfan LL14 22 E1
Eighth Av LL12 6 B3
Elder Cl LL12 7 F6
Eldon Gro LL14 15 H5
Eleventh Av LL12 6 B4
Ellice Way LL11 16 A2
Ellis St LL14 20 E1
Elm Ct LL12 8 C4
Elm Gro LL12 13 E6
Elm Grove Way LL12 13 E6
Elm Rd LL13 19 E2
Elm Walk LL12 6 B3
Elmanoak Gro LL12 6 B3
Elwyn Dr LL13 27 B2
Emlyn Ter LL14 20 D1
Emmanuel Gro LL14 22 D2
Empress Rd LL13 3 A5
Eneurys Rd LL11 12 D6
Enth Av LL12 6 B4
Epsom Way LL13 17 F5
Epworth Cl LL11 11 F2
Erddig Cl LL14 15 H6
Erddig Rd LL13 3 B6
Erlas Gro LL13 17 G2
Erlas La LL13 18 B1
Erlas Park Rd LL13 13 G6
Ernest Parry Rd LL13 17 G2
Erw Deg, Llangollen LL20 23 C6
Erw Deg, Wrexham LL14 21 A7
Erw Gaer LL11 11 F2
Erw Gerrig LL14 20 C2
Erw Las LL14 20 D3
Erw Lwyd LL14 20 C3
Erw Wladys LL20 26 C1
Esless La LL14 16 A5
Essex Cl LL11 12 D4
Estyn Cl LL12 4 C1
Ewart St LL14 24 D4
Eyton Grange LL12 7 F6

Fagl La LL12 4 A1
Faircroft Ct LL13 17 G5
Fairfield LL11 10 D2
Fairfield St LL13 3 C5
Fairmeadow CH4 8 F1
Fairmount Rd LL13 13 G6
Fairoaks Cres LL12 6 B3
Fairview, Holt LL13 27 B6
Fairview, Rhostyllen LL14 15 H5
Fairway Gdns LL11 11 H4
Fairy Rd LL13 3 B6
Falcon Rd LL13 17 G2
Farm Side LL12 13 F4
Farndon St LL12 3 D3
Farriers Walk LL12 7 F5
Felin Puleston LL13 16 A5
Fellows La LL12 4 B3
Fennant Rd LL14 20 E1
Fenwick Dr LL13 17 F2
Ferndale LL13 17 F2
Ferndale Av LL14 15 G6
Ferndale Rise LL11 12 A4
Fernham Dr LL13 13 E4
Fferm Llidiart Werdd LL11 10 A6
Ffordd Aeron LL11 10 B6
Ffordd Alafon LL12 13 F4
Ffordd Aled LL12 13 E4
Ffordd Almer LL12 12 D3
Ffordd Alun LL12 13 E4
Ffordd Bryn Madoc LL11 9 C3
Ffordd Caerfyrddin LL11 12 B5
Ffordd Cwm LL13 16 C5
Ffordd Cynan LL12 13 F4
Ffordd Dewi LL14 20 E3
Ffordd Dyfed, Rhosllanerchrugog LL14 20 D2
Ffordd Dyfed, Wrexham LL12 17 F1
Ffordd Dylan LL12 17 E1
Ffordd Edgeworth LL12 17 E1
Ffordd Eisteddfod LL11 9 B3
Ffordd Elan LL12 13 E5
Ffordd Elfed LL12 17 E1
Ffordd Elwy LL12 13 E5
Ffordd Estyn LL11 12 C4
Ffordd Frondeg LL13 16 D6
Ffordd Garmonydd LL12 12 D3
Ffordd Gerwyn LL13 16 D6
Ffordd Glyn LL13 16 C5
Ffordd Gryffydd LL12 6 A4
Ffordd Gwenllian LL12 6 C3
Ffordd Gwilym LL12 13 E6
Ffordd Gwynedd, Rhosllanerchrugog LL14 20 D3
Ffordd Gwynedd, Wrexham LL11 12 C5
Ffordd Hendre LL13 16 D6
Ffordd Hooson LL12 17 E1
Ffordd Ifor LL14 20 C4
Ffordd Iorwerth LL12 6 C3
Ffordd Isaf LL11 9 C3
Ffordd Jarvis LL12 13 E6
Ffordd Kayton LL14 22 E3
Ffordd Lerry LL12 13 E3
Ffordd Llanerch LL14 20 C4
Ffordd Llywelyn LL12 13 E3
Ffordd Mabon LL12 6 A4
Ffordd Maddoc LL12 6 A4
Ffordd Madoc LL12 13 E4
Ffordd Maelor LL12 17 E1
Ffordd Mailyn LL13 16 D5
Ffordd Meirionydd LL11 12 C5
Ffordd Mon LL11 12 C5
Ffordd Morgan, Llay LL12 6 A4
Ffordd Morgan, Wrexham LL12 12 D3
Ffordd Morgannwg LL11 12 C5
Ffordd Mynydd Isa LL14 20 C3
Ffordd Newydd LL11 9 C2
Ffordd Offa, Cefn-mawr LL14 22 E3
Ffordd Offa, Rhosllanerchrugog LL14 20 E3
Ffordd Owain, Brymbo LL11 10 D2
Ffordd Owain, Wrexham LL12 13 E3
Ffordd Pedrog LL12 13 F4
Ffordd Pentre LL14 20 F2
Ffordd Powell LL11 15 G1
Ffordd Powys LL14 20 D3
Ffordd Tegid LL12 13 F4
Ffordd Tegla LL12 13 E4
Ffordd Trefaldwyn LL11 12 C5
Ffordd Trefin LL12 13 F4
Ffordd Tudno LL12 13 E4
Ffordd Ty Mawr LL14 22 E3
Ffordd Tyn y Cestyll Rd LL20 26 B3
Ffordd Uchaf LL11 9 C3
Ffordd y Gaer LL11 12 B1
Ffordd Yr Ysgol LL11 9 C3
Ffordd Ystrad LL13 16 C5
Ffrwd Rd LL12 5 B6
Field Vw LL13 17 E2
Fifth Av LL12 6 B3
Finney Cl LL11 12 B5
Fir Tree Rd LL11 12 B1
Firgrove Cnr LL12 13 F5
First Av, Llay LL12 6 A3
First Av, Summerhill LL11 11 G2
First Av, Wrexham Ind Est LL13 19 E3
Five Crosses Ind Est LL11 10 A5
Fleming Dr LL11 12 B6
Fontwell Cl LL13 17 G5
Forest Pines LL13 13 H6
Forest Rd LL12 6 B3
Forge Cl LL11 11 F6
Forge Rd LL11 11 F5
Foster Rd LL11 3 C1
Foundry Rd LL13 3 C4
Fourth Av, Gwersyllt LL11 11 H3
Fourth Av, Llay LL12 6 A3
Fourth Rd LL13 19 E2
Foxwood Dr LL14 16 A4
Frances Av LL12 12 D4
Francis La, Holt LL13 27 A6
Francis La, Wrexham LL13 18 D1
Francis Rd LL11 11 F2
Fredrick St LL14 20 E2
Friars Cl LL12 13 E4
Friars Ct LL13 26 C4
Friars Mws LL13 26 C4
Frog La, Holt LL13 27 A5
Frog La, Wrexham LL13 17 G5
Fron Bache LL20 23 B5
Fron Castell LL20 23 B5
Fron Las LL11 14 B1
Fronheulog Hill LL11 9 C2
Furnace Cl LL11 10 D1
Furnace Rd LL12 5 B7

Gabriel Cl LL13 13 G6
Gainsborough Rd LL12 13 F5
Galaxy Gro LL11 11 G5
Gamford La LL12 8 F3
Gardd Estyn LL11 12 D5
Gardd Francis LL14 20 A4
Gardden Ind Est LL14 21 E5
Gardden Rd LL14 20 E2
Gardden Vw LL14 21 F5
Garden Ct, Rhosllanerchrugog LL14 20 D2
Garden Ct, Wrexham LL11 12 D5
Garden Rd LL11 3 B1
Garner Rd LL13 17 E2
Gate Rd LL20 22 B2
Gatefield LL13 16 D4
Gateway LL12 12 D6
Gatewen Rd LL11 11 G5
Gedington Cl LL13 13 H5
Gegin Rd LL11 9 F3
Gele Av LL11 12 A2
George Av LL20 22 B1
George St, Chirk LL14 24 D4
George St, Llangollen LL20 23 B4
George St, Wrexham LL11 3 B1
Ger y Ddol LL20 23 A4
Gerald St LL11 3 B1
Gerddi LL14 20 C1
Gibson St LL13 3 A4
Gladwyn Rd LL12 12 D4
Glan Aber LL12 17 E1
Glan Aber Cl LL11 12 A3
Glan Garth LL12 17 E2
Glan Gors LL13 17 G3
Glan Llyn Rd LL11 12 A2
Glanrafon LL14 20 C2
Glas Coed Way LL11 11 H4
Glasfryn LL14 20 F2
Glaslyn LL14 21 C8
Glen Avon LL12 17 E1
Gleneagles LL13 17 G1
Gloucester Dr LL11 16 A1
Glyn Av LL12 13 E5
Glyndwr Rd LL12 12 D5
Glyon La LL12 5 A8
Goodwood Gro LL13 17 F5
Gorse Cres LL12 7 F5
Goulbourne Av LL13 13 G6
Gourton Sq LL13 13 G5
Graigwen Rd LL11 11 F3
Grange Av LL11 12 C6
Grange Cl LL12 13 E5
Grange Rd LL20 23 B5
Grango La LL14 20 D1
Greek Rd LL14 20 D1
Green Cl LL14 22 E1
Green Ct LL11 11 E1
Green La, Llangollen LL20 23 B4
Green La, Wrexham LL14 24 F3
Green Mdws LL11 15 G1
Green Pk LL13 16 B5
Green Rd LL11 11 E1
Green St LL13 27 B5
Greenbank St LL13 3 D5
Greenfield LL11 16 C1
Greenfield Rd LL11 10 B6
Greenway CH3 27 C4
Greenway Vw LL12 7 E5
Greenways LL13 17 G5
Grenadin Cl LL11 11 G5
Gresford Ind Pk LL12 12 D2
Gresford Pk LL12 7 E5

Sibbersfield La CH3 27 D4
Silverbirch Dr LL12 7 F5
Sixth Av LL12 6 B4
Smelt La LL11 10 A6
Smelt Rd LL11 10 A6
Smith St LL14 20 C2
Smithfield Dr LL13 27 A6
Smithfield Grn LL13 27 B6
Smithfield Rd LL13 3 D4
Smithfield St LL13 27 B6
Smithy La LL12 12 D3
Smithy Rd LL11 11 E6
Snowdon Dr,
Johnstown LL14 20 F3
Snowdon Dr,
Wrexham LL11 12 C4
Sontley Rd LL13 3 B6
South La LL14 20 D1
South Vw, Chirk LL14 24 D4
South Vw,
Gresford LL12 7 E6
South Vw, Pandy LL11 12 C3
Southleigh Dr LL11 12 C5
Southsea Ind Est
LL11 11 E5
Southsea Rd LL11 11 F6
Spectrum Bsns Pk
LL13 18 D5
Speeds Way CH3 27 B4
Spinney Walk LL14 21 E7
Spring Gdns LL11 3 B1
Spring Rd,
Rhostyllen LL11 15 G6
Spring Rd,
Wrexham LL11 16 C1
Springfield Ct LL12 7 E5
Springfield La LL12 6 D5
Stablegates LL14 20 F2
Stabler Cres LL11 12 C4
Stables Rd LL11 11 F1
Stancliffe Av LL12 7 G5
Stanley Gro LL14 21 F6
Stanley Rd LL14 20 E1
Stanley St LL11 16 D4
Stansty Chain Rd LL11 12 A4
Stansty Cl LL11 12 B6
Stansty Dr LL11 12 B6
Stansty Lodge Rd LL11 12 A5
Stansty Rd LL11 12 B5
Starling Cl CH3 27 D4
Station App LL11 3 B1
Station Av LL14 25 C6
Station Ct LL11 12 A2
Station Rd,
Bangor-on-Dee LL13 26 C4
Station Rd, Chirk LL14 25 C6
Station Rd,
Llangollen LL20 22 B1
Station Rd,
Marchwiel LL13 27 C2
Station Rd,
Pentre Broughton LL11 11 E2
Station Rd,
Rhostyllen LL14 15 G5
Station Rd,
Rossett LL12 8 C4
Station Rd,
Ruabon LL14 21 E7
Station Ter LL14 21 F7
Steam Cl LL11 10 D2
Steel Cl LL11 10 D2
Stephens La*,
School Rd LL14 20 C2
Stirling Av LL11 12 C5
Stockwell Gro LL13 16 D5
Stonewalls LL12 8 B3
Straight Mile LL12 6 B2
Stratford Cl LL12 13 E6
Stretton Cl LL13 16 D6
Stryt Isa LL14 20 B3
Stryt Las LL14 20 D3
Stryt Maelor LL11 9 D1
Stryt y Bydden LL11 15 G1
Stryt y Scwelar LL11 14 A2
Stuart St LL13 3 D6
Stuart Way LL13 3 D6
Summerfields LL14 15 H5
Summerhill Rd LL11 11 G3
Sun La LL13 19 G6
Sunhill Dr LL12 4 C3
Sunningdale Cl LL13 13 G6
Sunny Vw LL11 11 H2
Sunnyacre LL11 12 A3
Sunnyhill LL11 11 G5
Sunnyridge LL14 7 G4
Sussex Gdns LL11 12 D4

Sutton Dr LL13 17 G1
Swan St LL14 20 C1
Sycamore Dr,
Chirk LL14 24 E3
Sycamore Dr,
Gresford LL12 7 F5
Sycamore Rd LL13 17 F2
Sylester Ct LL13 17 E5

Tabor Hill LL11 14 B1
Tai Chapel*,
Summerhill Rd LL11 11 G3
Talbot Ct LL13 3 C6
Talbot Rd LL13 3 C6
Taliesin LL13 27 B1
Talwrn Rd LL11 10 A6
Tan Llan La LL11 14 D1
Tan y Bryn,
Rhosllanerchrugog
LL14 20 D3
Tan y Bryn,
Wrexham LL13 17 F3
Tan y Clawdd LL14 20 F2
Tan y Coed,
Johnstown LL14 20 F1
Tan y Coed,
Llangollen LL20 23 C6
Tan y Coed,
Wrexham LL13 17 G5
Tan y Ddol LL20 23 A4
Tan yr Allt LL12 5 C7
Tanat Way LL13 17 G3
Tanydre LL13 17 F1
Tanyfron Rd LL11 10 C5
Tanylan LL14 21 F7
Tapley Av LL12 13 F5
Tatham Rd LL14 21 E6
Taunton Cl LL13 3 B5
Tegan LL14 20 F2
Tegfan Ct*,
High St LL12 4 B3
Tegid Ct LL14 21 C8
Tegid Dr LL11 11 G6
Telford Av,
Llangollen LL20 22 B2
Telford Av,
Wrexham LL14 25 D8
Temperance Rd LL11 11 E5
Temple Row LL13 3 C4
Tenters Cl LL14 3 B4
Tenters Sq LL13 3 B4
Tenth Av LL12 6 B4
Terrig Way LL11 11 H4
The Beeches,
Hope LL12 4 C1
The Beeches,
Wrexham LL12 12 D6
The Beechlands LL12 13 E6
The Belvedere LL11 9 D1
The Brambles LL11 11 G6
The Bridgeway Centre
LL13 18 C4
The Conifers LL12 7 E5
The Copse LL12 8 C4
The Crofts CH3 27 C5
The Cross LL13 27 B5
The Glen LL13 27 B2
The Green LL13 12 D4
The Groves LL13 27 C2
The Haven LL14 20 E1
The Hawthorns LL12 13 E6
The Homestead LL14 16 A4
The Larches*,
Park St LL14 20 E2
The Laurels LL12 13 E6
The Limes LL12 8 D4
The Links LL13 13 H5
The Meadows LL11 12 A4
The Millyard LL12 8 E2
The Mount LL12 17 E1
The Nurseries,
Chirk LL14 25 E5
The Nurseries,
Gresford LL12 7 E6
The Oaks LL14 20 B3
The Old Gdns LL13 17 G1
The Orchards,
Holt LL13 27 B5
The Orchards,
Rossett LL12 8 E3
The Orchards,
Wrexham LL13 17 F5
The Oval LL13 18 C5
The Paddocks LL11 14 C1
The Parks LL11 10 D5
The Pines LL12 12 D6

The Pinfold LL13 27 B5
The Rest LL14 22 E2
The Ridgeway LL13 27 C2
The Small Woods LL14 21 E7
The Spinney,
Gwynfryn LL11 9 D3
The Spinney,
Marford LL12 7 F2
The Sycamores LL11 11 G2
The Triangle LL13 13 G5
The Willows LL12 12 D6
Third Av,
Gwersyllt LL11 11 H3
Third Av, Llay LL12 6 A3
Thirlmere Ct LL11 12 A2
Thistledown Ct LL14 15 H5
Thomas Ct LL13 17 E5
Thornhill Dr LL14 16 A4
Thornhurst Dr LL13 13 H6
Thornleigh LL13 17 G1
Thornleigh Dr LL12 7 F5
Top Rd LL11 11 G1
Tower Cl LL13 19 E3
Tower Rd LL20 23 A3
Tower Vw LL13 17 F2
Town Hill LL13 3 C4
Townfield Av CH3 27 B4
Townfield La CH3 27 B4
Townsend Av LL12 13 F5
Trafalgar LL13 16 D4
Trehowell Av LL14 25 D8
Trem Dolydd LL14 22 D2
Trem Eryri LL11 12 C5
Trem y Berwyn LL14 20 C4
Trem y Gardden LL14 20 C4
Trem y Gwernant LL20 23 C5
Trem y Mynydd LL11 9 F4
Trem y Nant LL11 11 F3
Trem yr Eglwys LL13 16 C5
Trem yr Ysgol LL20 23 C6
Trem y Nant LL13 16 C5
Trevalyn Hall Vw LL12 8 E4
Trevalyn Way LL12 8 D4
Trevenna Way LL13 17 E2
Trevor Av LL14 15 H6
Trevor Rd,
Llangollen LL20 23 D4
Trevor Rd,
Wrexham LL14 25 D6
Trevor St LL13 3 C6
Treweryn Cl LL12 6 A4
Trident Way LL13 13 G5
Trinity Cl LL14 15 G6
Trinity St,
Rhostyllen LL14 15 H6
Trinity St,
Wrexham LL11 3 C3
Trofryn LL14 20 C4
Troon Cl LL13 13 G6
Tryweryn Pl LL13 17 G3
Tudor Av,
Gwersyllt LL11 12 A2
Tudor Av,
Rhostyllen LL14 15 G6
Tudor Ct, Hope LL12 4 B1
Tudor Ct,
Johnstown LL14 20 F2
Tudor Rd LL13 16 D5
Tudor St LL11 10 A6
Turnberry Av LL13 13 H6
Turner Cl LL13 13 G6
Turnpike La LL12 7 F4
Tuttle St LL13 3 C4
Ty Cerrig Dr LL12 4 B3
Ty Gwyn La LL11 11 G5
Ty Newydd Ct LL14 21 F7
Ty Wesley*,
Australia St LL14 20 D1
Tyn Dwr Rd LL20 23 D5
Tyn y Celyn Dr LL20 23 D5
Tyn y Plas LL20 23 A5

Union Rd LL13 3 A2

Vale Vw,
Wrexham LL12 6 B5
Vale Vw, Wrexham LL11 11 F5
Valley Way LL13 16 D5
Vauxhall Ind Est
LL14 20 F4
Vernon St LL11 3 B2
Vicarage Cl LL11 11 G2
Vicarage St LL13 27 B5
Vicarage Hill,
Minera LL11 9 F4

Vicarage Hill,
Rhostyllen LL14 15 G6
Vicarage Hill,
Wrexham LL13 3 C4
Vicarage La LL12 7 E6
Vicarage Rd LL20 23 B5
Victoria Av LL14 20 E2
Victoria Rd,
Brynteg LL11 11 F5
Victoria Rd,
Coedpoeth LL11 14 B1
Victoria Rd,
Wrexham LL13 3 A5
Victoria St LL14 20 D2
Victory Pl LL12 6 B4
Viking Cl LL11 11 H3
Village Cl LL11 12 D5
Village Mdw LL14 21 F7
Village Walks LL12 7 G3
Villiers St LL13 3 A4
Vincent St LL14 21 F6
Vinegar Hill LL14 20 D1
Vron Cl LL11 10 D2
Vyrnwy Cl LL11 11 H4
Vyrnwy Way LL13 17 G3

Waen Rd LL11 10 B6
Walden Cres LL14 25 E5
Walker Cl LL13 13 G6
Walkers La,
Farndon CH3 27 C4
Walkers La,
Rhosllanerchrugog
LL14 20 D1
Walnut Cotts LL13 27 B5
Walnut Gro LL12 6 B3
Walnut St LL11 16 C1
Waring Ct LL13 17 E5
Warrenwood Rd LL12 13 F5
Warwick Av LL13 17 E4
Waterloo Cl LL13 16 D5
Watery Rd LL13 3 A3
Wats Dyke Way LL11 12 C4
Watts Dyke LL14 6 A4
Wavell Rd LL13 17 E3
Waverley Cres LL12 8 E3
Waynnstay Ind Est
LL14 21 D7
Weale Ct LL13 17 E5
Well St LL14 22 D2
Wellington Rd LL13 3 B5
Wellswood Rd LL13 13 E3
Wenfryn Cl LL20 22 B1
Wens St LL14 20 C1
Wentworth Rise LL13 13 H6
Wern LL14 24 D4
Wern La LL14 20 D2
Wern Las LL14 20 D3
Wern Rd,
Llangollen LL20 23 B4
Wern Rd,
Wrexham LL13 9 E4
Wesley Rd LL11 9 C1
West Bank Rd LL12 6 A3
West Circle LL13 17 E2
West Gro LL14 15 G6
West St,
Llangollen LL20 23 B4
West St, Wrexham LL11 16 B1
West Way LL12 8 E4
Westbourne Dr LL14 15 H5
Westbury Dr LL11 12 C3
Western Vw LL11 12 C3
Westfield Ct LL13 17 G5
Westminster Cl LL12 16 D1
Westminster Dr,
Gresford LL12 7 F5
Westminster Dr,
Wrexham LL12 16 D1
Westminster Rd LL11 11 F2
Weston Dr LL11 12 B6
Weston Rd LL11 15 G1
Westwood Dr LL13 13 G6
Whalleys Way LL14 21 B8
Wharf Hill LL20 23 B4
Wheat Cl LL11 11 H4
Wheatsheaf La LL11 11 G3
Wheatsheaf Mws LL11 11 H3
Whitchurch Rd LL13 26 C5
White Lion Cl LL11 11 G2
White Oaks LL11 9 D1
Whitegate Flds LL13 27 B5
Whitegate Light Ind Est
LL13 17 F4
Whitegate Rd LL11 17 E4
Whitehurst Link LL14 24 D2

Whiteway Dr LL12 7 E...
Whitland Way LL13 17 F...
Wilkinson Dr LL14 15 G...
William St LL14 20 E...
Williams Ter LL14 20 E...
Williams Way LL12 8 D...
Willow Av LL12 4 C...
Willow Ct,
Bangor-on-Dee LL13 26 C...
Willow Ct,
Wrexham LL13 17 G...
Willow Dr,
Gresford LL12 7 F...
Willow Dr, Llay LL12 6 B...
Willow Lea Cl LL11 12 A...
Willow Rd LL11 10 B...
Willow St LL20 23 B...
Wilson Av LL13 17 E...
Winchester Way LL12 7 F...
Windermere Rd LL12 12 D...
Windrush Cl LL13 17 E...
Windsor Av LL12 4 A...
Windsor Dr LL11 16 B...
Windsor Rd,
New Broughton LL11 11 G...
Windsor Rd,
Rhosllanerchrugog
LL14 20 D...
Woburn Cl LL13 17 G...
Woodberry Cl LL14 16 A...
Woodland Gro,
Llangollen LL20 22 C...
Woodland Gro,
Wrexham LL13 17 F...
Woodland Rd LL11 11 F...
Woodlands Ct LL11 10 D...
Woodlands Rd,
Llangollen LL20 22 B...
Woodlands Rd,
Wrexham LL12 7 F...
Woodridge Av LL12 7 F...
Woodside Ct LL14 15 H...
Woodwards Walk LL14 21 C...
Worcester Rd LL13 26 C...
Worsley Av LL14 20 F...
Wrexham Bsns Pk
LL13 18 D...
Wrexham By Pass 15 G...
Wrexham Ind Est
LL13 19 F...
Wrexham Rd,
Brynteg LL11 11 G...
Wrexham Rd,
Caergwrle LL12 4 B...
Wrexham Rd,
Chester LL12,CH4 8 E...
Wrexham Rd,
Holt LL13 27 A...
Wrexham Rd,
Rhostyllen LL14 15 G...
Wrexham Rd,
Wrexham LL13 13 H...
Wyndam Gdns LL13 17 G...
Wyndham Dr LL12 5 C...
Wynn Av, Ruabon LL14 21 F...
Wynn Av,
Wrexham LL11 12 C...
Wynnstay Av LL13 17 F...
Wynnstay Cres LL14 15 H...
Wynnstay La LL12 7 G...

Y Berllan LL11 10 A...
Y Fron LL14 20 F...
Y Gamer LL20 26 C...
Y Gesail LL14 20 F...
Y Gorlan LL12 20 D...
Y Maes LL20 26 C...
Y Stryt Fawr LL11 14 B...
Y Wern LL13 17 F...
Yale Gro LL12 12 D...
Yale Pk LL11 16 B...
Yale St LL14 20 E...
Yarwood Dr LL13 13 E...
Yew Tree Ct LL12 7 E...
York Cl LL13 17 G...
Yorke Av LL13 27 B...
Yorke Cl LL13 27 C...
Yorke St LL13 3 D...
Yr Helfa LL14 24 E...